Title - Profit-C from Prophecies of War
ISBN 13 - 978-1-955144-10-0
Composer - Andrew T Hanna
Graphic Design, Layout, & Artwork - Andrew T Hanna
Copyright - 2022
Genre - Progressive Rock, Jazz-Fusion, Jazz-Rock

Profit=C

from Prophecies of War

Composed By - Andrew Hanna

Artwork & Layout - Andrew Hanna

ISBN (13) - 978-1-955144-10-0

Genre - Jazz-Rock, Jazz Fusion, Prog-Rock

Profit=C
began to take shape
in April 2001 with completion
in the fall of that year. It, like many
other of my compositions, began as a musical
challenge. The challenge was to create two
diametrically opposed melodies. The first melody is a melodic
phrase based in B Aeolian that opens Profit=C. And the
second phrase is a repetitive 8th note phrase that alternates between E minor
triad and Bb major seventh. The second aspect of the musical challenge was to
build a bridge that would slowly transform the first melody into the second melody. As the
transformations began to take shape, the ante was upped and different musical voices were added to
create a sea of melodic voices.

At that time in my musical development I was fascinated by rounds and cannons. The fascination stems from how
composers of yore could create a single melody and have that melody enter at different times without it creating
unwanted dissonances.

In the end, I'm quite happy with how Profit=C went from two simple melodies and were developed into a much
larger composition. When we first rehearsed this song, it took a few attempts for the musicians to gain confidence
of having others perform the same melody at different times. Only to have that melody transform and merge
into a single repetitive phrase.

And with all that said . . . enjoy.

Andrew Hanna

Score

Profit-C

Andrew Hanna

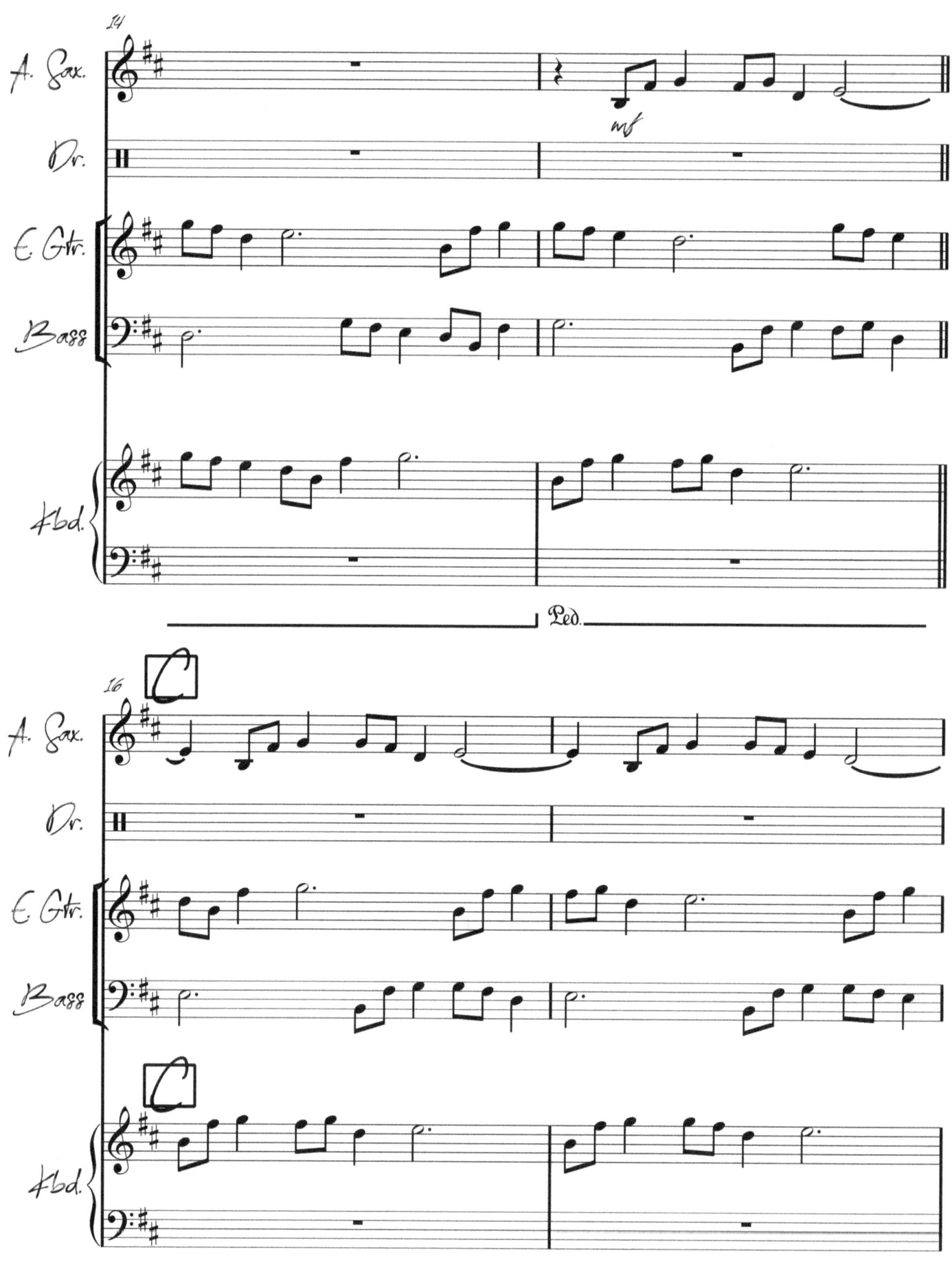

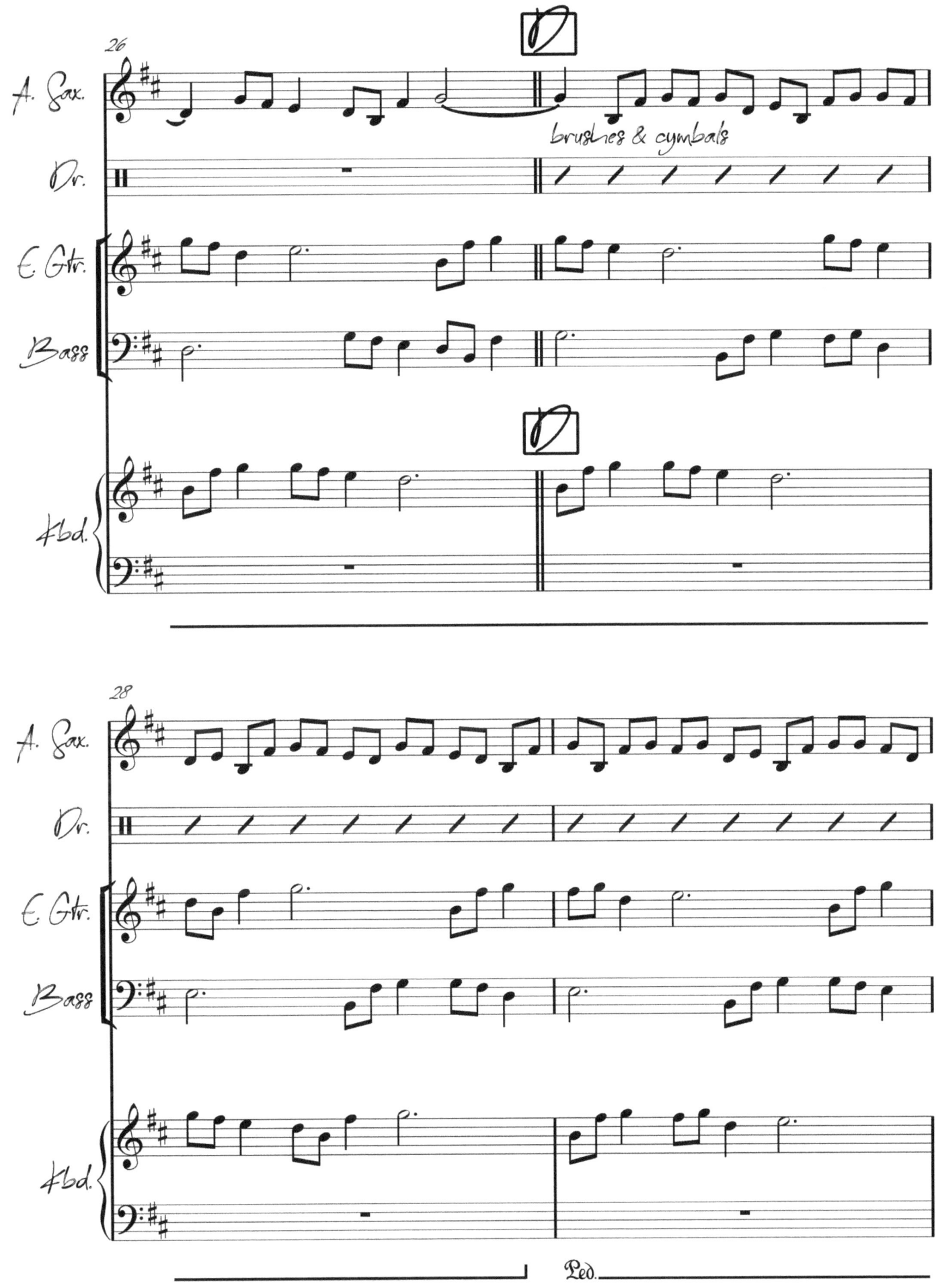

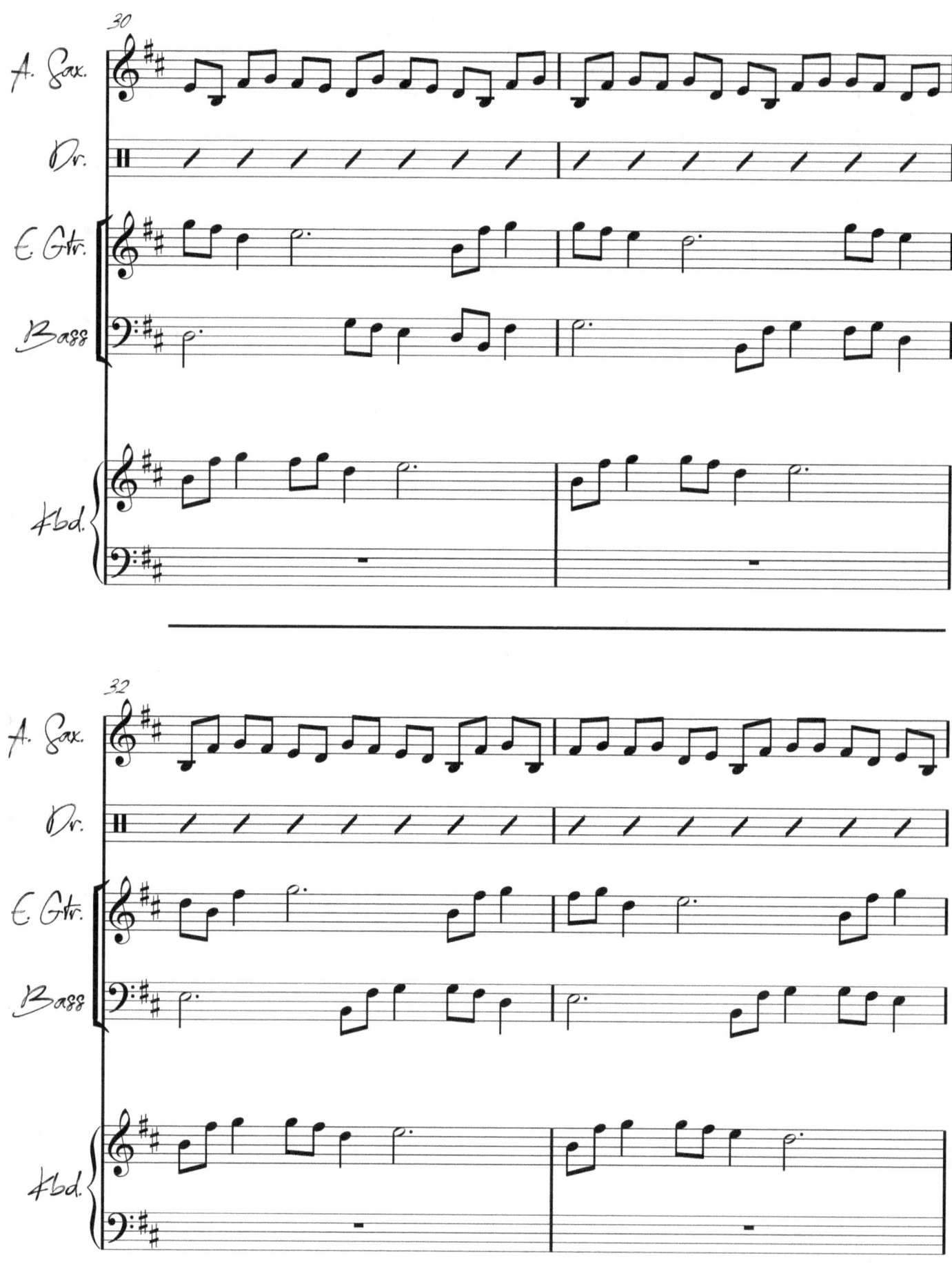

Alto Saxophone

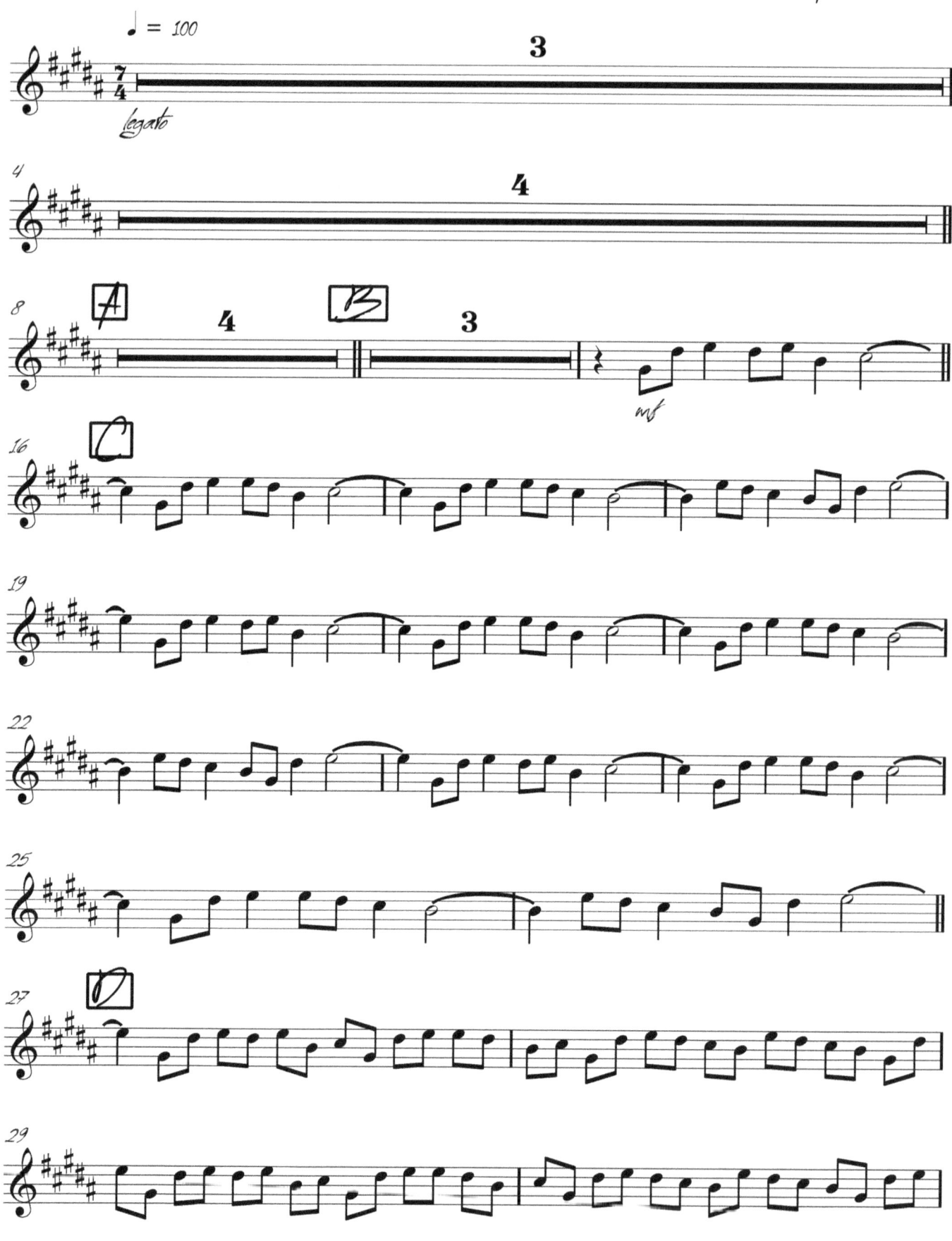

Alto Sax

Bass Guitar

Bass Guitar

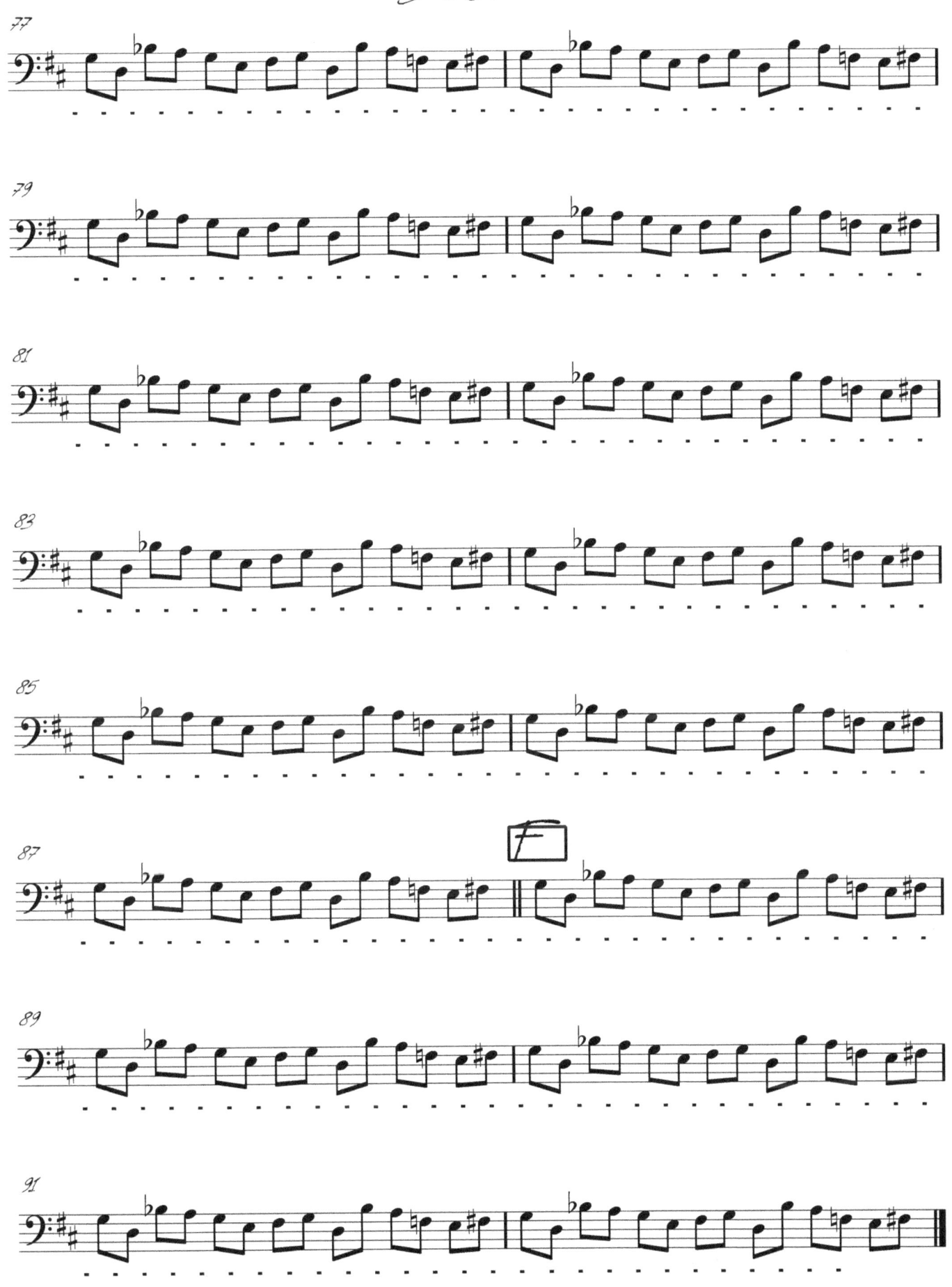

Bass Guitar

Drum Set

Drum Set

Profit=C

Andrew Hanna

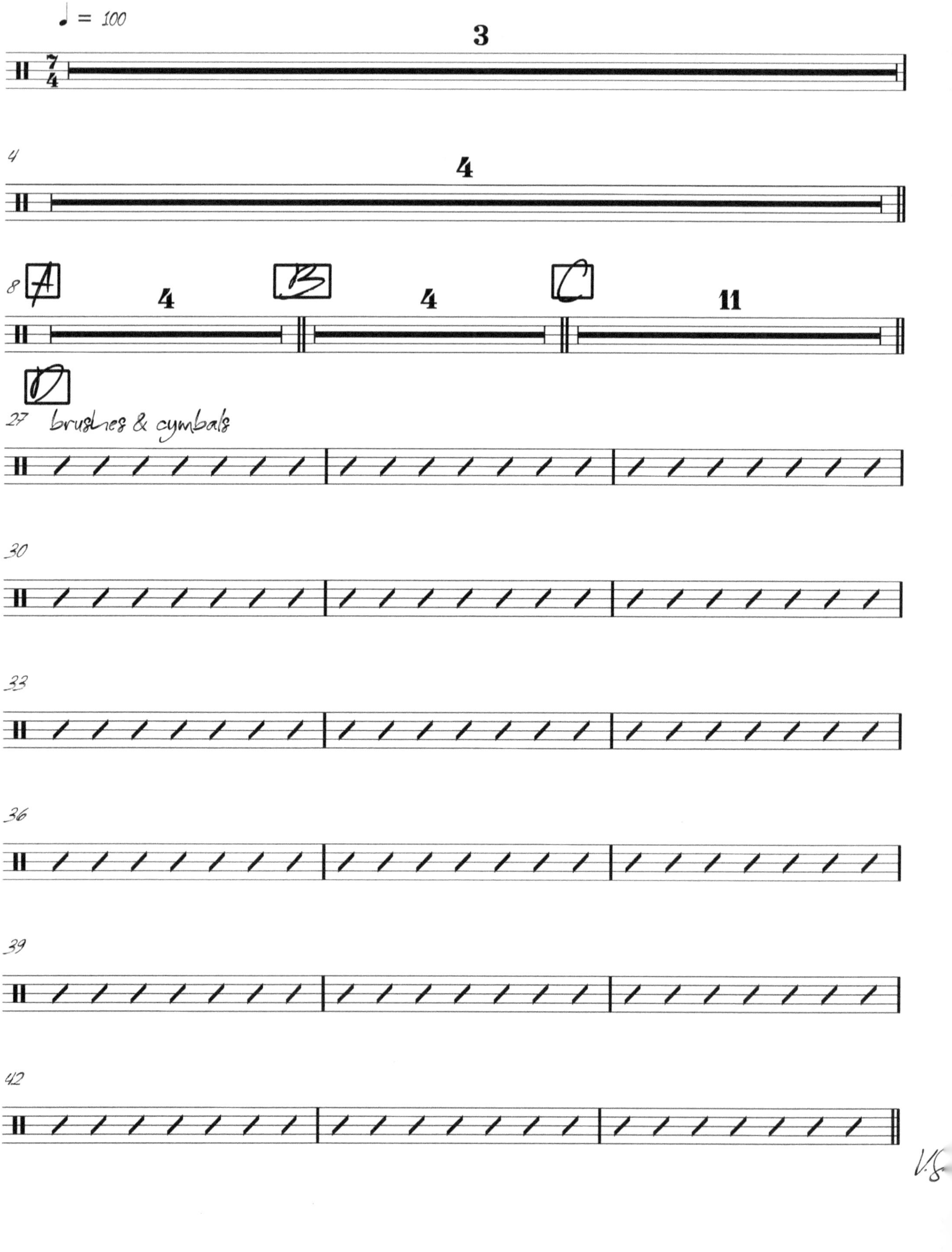

♩ = 100

3

| 7/4 |

4

4

8 A **4** B **4** C **11**

D

27 brushes & cymbals

30

33

36

39

42

V.S

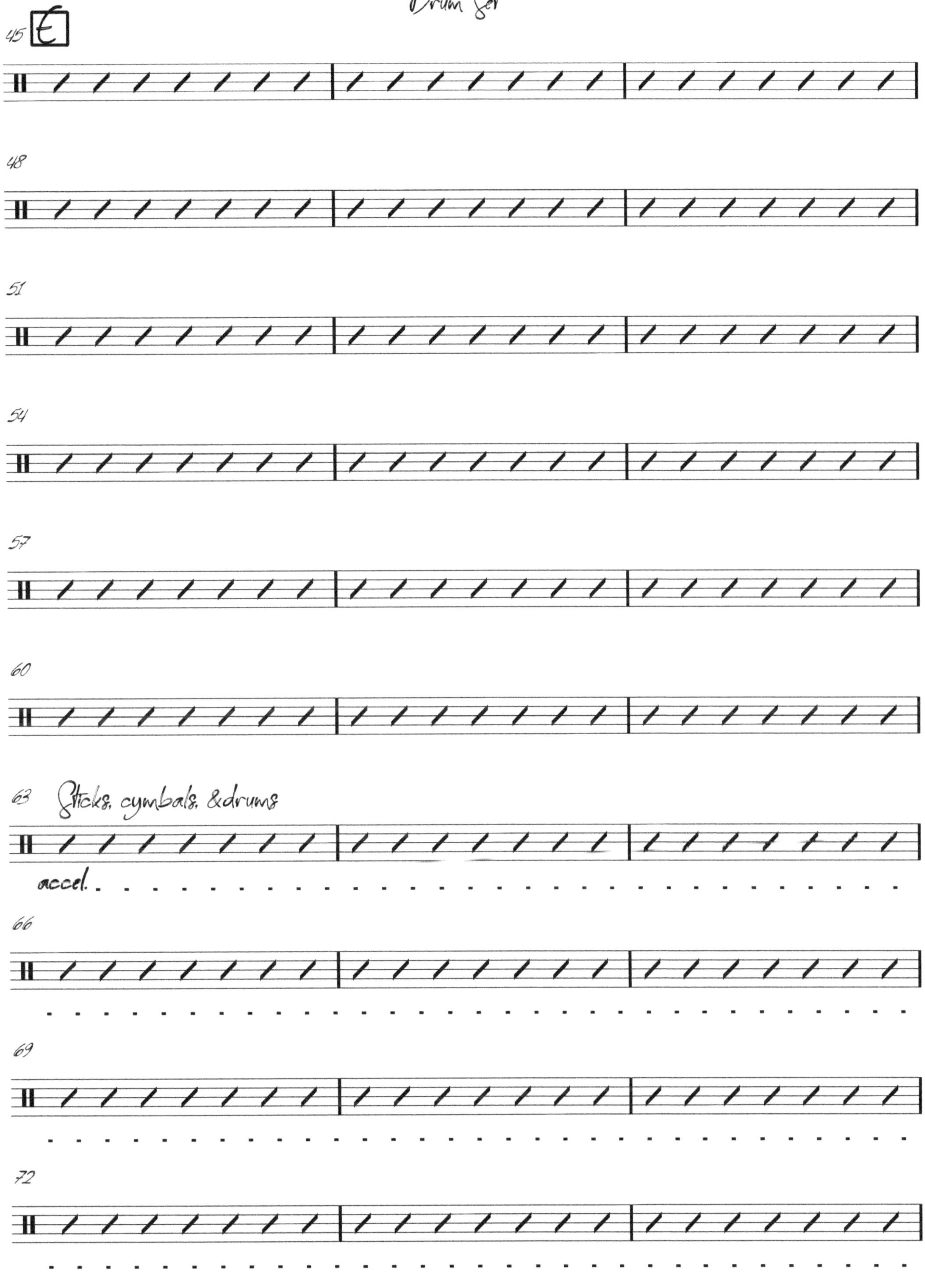

45 **E**

48

51

54

57

60

63 Sticks, cymbals, &drums

accel. . . . .

66

. . . .

69

. . . .

72

. . . .

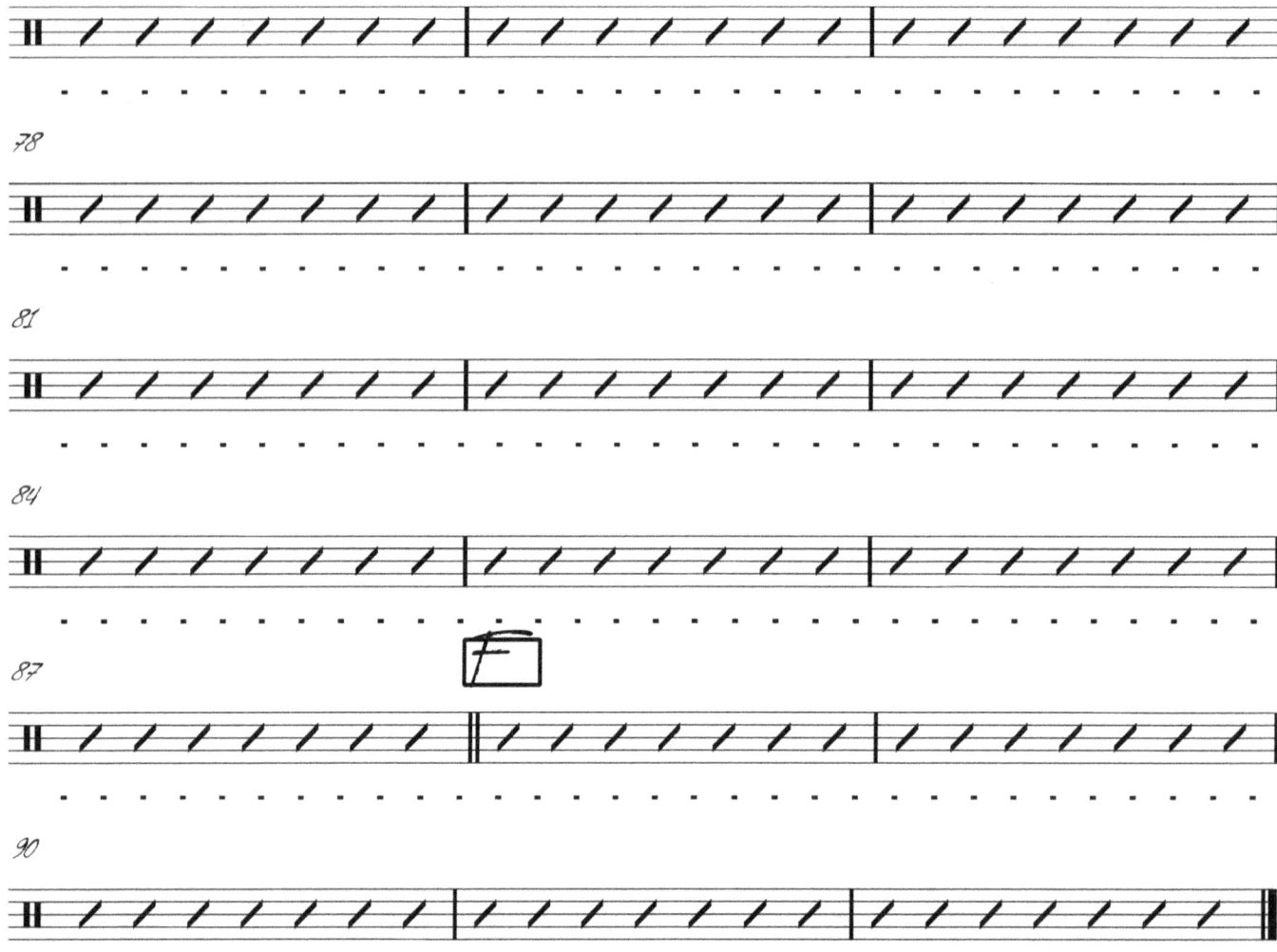

Electric Guitar

Electric Guitar

Electric Guitar

Keyboards

Profit-C

Keyboard

Andrew Hanna

Keyboard

Keyboard

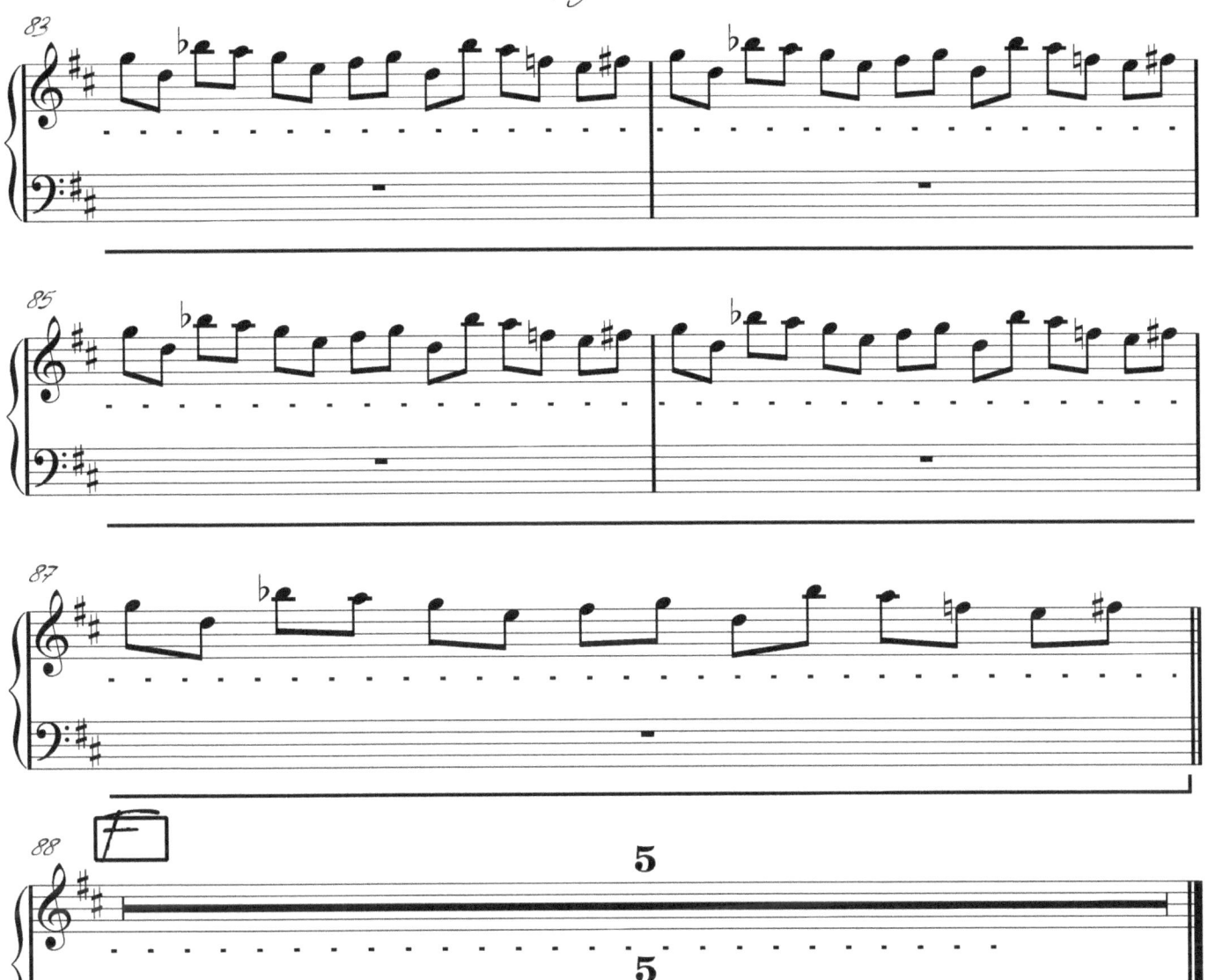

LEVEL 8 Supplemental

EXAM SERIES

By Glory St. Germain ARCT RMT MYCC UMTC &
Shelagh McKibbon-U'Ren RMT UMTC

ULTIMATE
MUSIC THEORY

GSG MUSIC

Enriching Lives Through Music Education

ISBN: 978-1-990358-17-3

The Ultimate Music Theory™ Program

Enriching Lives Through Music Education

The Ultimate Music Theory™ Workbooks & Answer Books Program includes:

UMT Rudiments Workbooks for Prep 1, Prep 2, Basic, Intermediate, Advanced & Complete
UMT Exam Series (Set #1 & Set #2) for Preparatory, Basic, Intermediate & Advanced

Supplemental Workbooks for PREP LEVEL, LEVELS 1 - 8 & COMPLETE LEVEL
UMT Supplemental Exam Series for LEVEL 5, LEVEL 6, LEVEL 7 & LEVEL 8

The Ultimate Music Theory Program is the *Way to Score Success* as UMT helps students prepare for nationally recognized theory examinations including the Royal Conservatory of Music.

Library and Archives Canada Cataloguing in Publication. UMT Workbooks & Exam Series /Glory St. Germain & Shelagh McKibbon-U'Ren. Respect Copyright. All rights reserved. GlorylandPublishing.com

Ultimate Music Theory Rudiments Exam Series

GP - EPS1	ISBN: 978-1-927641-00-2	Preparatory Rudiments Exams Set #1
GP - EPS1A	ISBN: 978-1-927641-08-8	Preparatory Exams Answers Set #1
GP - EPS2	ISBN: 978-1-927641-01-9	Preparatory Rudiments Exams Set #2
GP - EPS2A	ISBN: 978-1-927641-09-5	Preparatory Exams Answers Set #2
GP - EBS1	ISBN: 978-1-927641-02-6	Basic Rudiments Exams Set #1
GP - EBS1A	ISBN: 978-1-927641-10-1	Basic Exams Answers Set #1
GP - EBS2	ISBN: 978-1-927641-03-3	Basic Rudiments Exams Set #2
GP - EBS2A	ISBN: 978-1-927641-11-8	Basic Exams Answers Set #2
GP - EIS1	ISBN: 978-1-927641-04-0	Intermediate Rudiments Exams Set #1
GP - EIS1A	ISBN: 978-1-927641-12-5	Intermediate Exams Answers Set #1
GP - EIS2	ISBN: 978-1-927641-05-7	Intermediate Rudiments Exams Set #2
GP - EIS2A	ISBN: 978-1-927641-13-2	Intermediate Exams Answers Set #2
GP - EAS1	ISBN: 978-1-927641-06-4	Advanced Rudiments Exams Set #1
GP - EAS1A	ISBN: 978-1-927641-14-9	Advanced Exams Answers Set #1
GP - EAS2	ISBN: 978-1-927641-07-1	Advanced Rudiments Exams Set #2
GP - EAS2A	ISBN: 978-1-927641-15-6	Advanced Exams Answers Set #2

Ultimate Music Theory Supplemental Exam Series

GP-L5E	ISBN: 978-1-990358-11-1	LEVEL 5 Exams
GP-L5EA	ISBN: 978-1-990358-12-8	LEVEL 5 Exams Answers
GP-L6E	ISBN: 978-1-990358-13-5	LEVEL 6 Exams
GP-L6EA	ISBN: 978-1-990358-14-2	LEVEL 6 Exams Answers
GP-L7E	ISBN: 978-1-990358-15-9	LEVEL 7 Exams
GP-L7EA	ISBN: 978-1-990358-16-6	LEVEL 7 Exams Answers
GP-L8E	ISBN: 978-1-990358-17-3	LEVEL 8 Exams
GP-L8EA	ISBN: 978-1-990358-18-0	LEVEL 8 Exams Answers

Go to UltimateMusicTheory.com **and check out the FREE Resources**

Ultimate Music Theory FREE RESOURCES created just for you!